W9-BIU-809

Animal Builders

A Rabbit's Burrow

Niles Worthington

Cavendish Square

New York

Published in 2017 by Cavendish Square Publishing, LLC
243 5th Avenue, Suite 136, New York, NY 10016

Copyright © 2017 by Cavendish Square Publishing, LLC

First Edition

Library of Congress Cataloging-in-Publication Data

Names: Worthington, Niles.
Title: A rabbit's burrow / Niles Worthington.
Description: New York : Cavendish Square, 2017. | Series: Animal builders | Includes index.
Identifiers: ISBN 9781502620866 (pbk.) | ISBN 9781502620880 (library bound) | ISBN 9781502620873 (6 pack) | ISBN 9781502620897 (ebook)
Subjects: LCSH: Rabbits--Habitations--Juvenile literature. | Animal burrowing--Juvenile literature. | Animal behavior--Juvenile literature.
Classification: LCC QL737.L32 W67 2017 | DDC 599.32--dc23

Editorial Director: David McNamara
Editor: Fletcher Doyle
Copy Editor: Rebecca Rohan
Assistant Art Director: Amy Greenan
Designer: Stephanie Flecha
Production Coordinator: Karol Szymczuk
Photo Research: J8 Media

The photographs in this book are used by permission and through the courtesy of:
Cover Tony Hamblin/Getty Images; p. 5 Paul Maguire/Shutterstock.com; p. 7, 19 Oxford Scientific/Getty Images; p. 9 Stan Osolinski/Getty Images; p. 11 Drakuliren/Shutterstock.com; p. 13 Philip Friskorn/NiS/Minden Pictures/Getty Images; p. 15 Steve Shott/Getty Images; p. 17 Edward Westmacott/Shutterstock.com; p. 21 Dimitris_K/Shutterstock.com.

Printed in the United States of America

Contents

Many rabbits live in burrows.
These are holes. Rabbits
dig them.

5

Burrows have rooms.
Some are for sleeping.

7

A female rabbit is a **doe**.
She builds the nest.
She uses grass.

She pulls out some fur.
This will warm her babies.
They are called **kits**.

11

Rabbits live in groups.
They form a **colony**.

13

Rabbits build tunnels.
They lead to other burrows.
This makes a **warren**.

15

A warren has many holes.
They help rabbits avoid
predators.

17

Rabbits add burrows for kits.
Warrens can get large.

19

Tunnels can be very long.
This makes room for
many rabbits.

New Words

colony (KAH-luh-nee) A group of people or animals living in the same spot.

doe (DOH) An adult female rabbit or deer. The adult male is a buck.

kit (KIT) A young animal, like a rabbit.

predators (PRE-duh-tors) Animals that hunt other animals.

warren (WORE-en) A group of burrows joined by tunnels.

Index

About the Author

Niles Worthington plays soccer and tennis and enjoys writing children's books. He works as a pharmacist and loves studying nature.

About BOOKWORMS

Bookworms help independent readers gain reading confidence through high-frequency words, simple sentences, and strong picture/text support. Each book explores a concept that helps children relate what they read to the world they live in.